BOOK 3 - Trombone

STANDARD OF EXCELLENCE

COMPREHENSIVE BAND METHOD

By Bruce Pearson

Dear Student:

Welcome to STANDARD OF EXCELLENCE Book 3.

By now, you have demonstrated that you are making steady progress toward becoming an accomplished musician. With the skills you are mastering on your instrument, you are beginning to realize the value of hard work and the joy of music-making.

STANDARD OF EXCELLENCE Book 3 introduces you to some of the world's finest music. By performing this literature, you will gain an appreciation for a variety of musical styles while improving your individual instrument and ensemble skills.

Best wishes as you explore Book 3.

Sincerely,

Bruce Pearson

Practicing - the key to EXCELLENCE!

▶ Make practicing part of your daily schedule. If you plan it as you do any other activity, you will find plenty of time for it.

▶ Try to practice in the same place every day. Choose a place where you can concentrate on making music. Start with a regular and familiar warm-up routine, including long tones and simple technical exercises. Like an athlete, you need to warm-up your mind and muscles before you begin performing.

▶ Set goals for every practice session. Keep track of your practice time and progress on the front cover Practice Journal.

▶ Practice the hard spots in your lesson assignments and band music over and over, until you can play them perfectly.

▶ At the end of each practice session, play something fun.

ISBN 0-8497-5987-0

KJOS NEIL A. KJOS MUSIC COMPANY, PUBLISHER

W23TB

REVIEW	Bb MAJOR KEY SIGNATURE	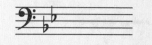
STYLE	*simile* - Continue playing in the same manner.	

1 **WARM-UP - Band Arrangement**

Andante

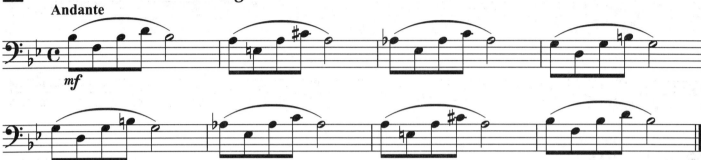

▶ Plan where to take breaths.

2 **TECHNIQUE BREAK**

Moderato

simile

3 **RIG A JIG JIG**

American Folk Song

Moderato

4 **TECHNIQUE BREAK**

Allegretto

simile

REVIEW

G MINOR
KEY SIGNATURE

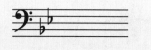

5 **G MINOR SCALE SKILL**
Moderato

Natural Minor

Harmonic Minor

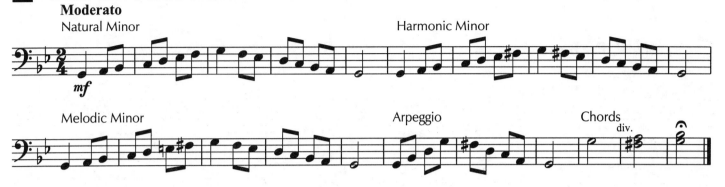

Melodic Minor

Arpeggio

Chords
div.

6 **PAT-A-PAN**
Moderato div.

French Carol

7 **INTERVAL INQUISITION**

div.   unis.   div.   unis.   div.   unis.   div.

▶ Write in the intervals on the lines provided.

8 **ARTICULATION ADVENTURE**
Allegretto

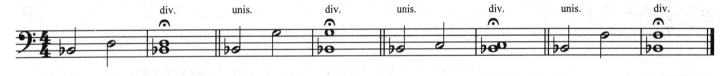

9 **GO FOR EXCELLENCE!**
Allegro

1.

2.

▶ Lines with a medal are *Achievement Lines*. The chart on the inside back cover can be used to record your progress.

| REVIEW | Eb MAJOR KEY SIGNATURE | 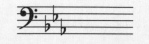 |

| MAJOR CHORD | 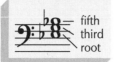 fifth third root | MINOR CHORD | 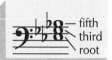 fifth third root |

| DYNAMICS | *fortissimo (**ff**) -* very loud   *pianissimo (**pp**) -* very soft |

10 DYNAMIC DYNAMICS

11 MAJOR AND MINOR CHORD EAR TRAINER

▶ Sing before you play.

12 TECHNIQUE BREAK

13 MY PARTNER AND I

Swedish Folk Dance

14 FOR TROMBONES ONLY

   Page 44 ▶

▶ When you see a page number followed by an arrow, *Excellerate* to the page indicated for additional studies.

REVIEW

**F MAJOR
KEY SIGNATURE**

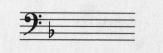

20 **WARM-UP - Band Arrangement**

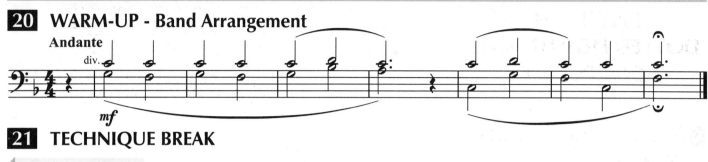

21 **TECHNIQUE BREAK**

▶ Try playing both octaves.

22 **THE BRITISH GRENADIERS**

English Folk Song

▶ Try to breathe only at the end of phrases.

23 **FOR TROMBONES ONLY**   Page 44 ▥▥▥▶

W23TB

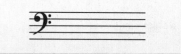

REVIEW | **C MAJOR KEY SIGNATURE**

SIXTEENTH/ DOTTED EIGHTH NOTE COMBINATION

24 C MAJOR SCALE SKILL

Moderato — Arpeggio — Chords div.

25 ARTICULATION ADVENTURE

Andante

clap

▶ Write in the counting for the top line before you play.

26 GREEN GROW THE RASHES O

Scottish Folk Song

Moderato

27 TECHNIQUE BREAK

Andante

28 GO FOR EXCELLENCE!

Scottish Folk Song

Andante
"Bonnie Glen Shee"

REVIEW	Ab MAJOR KEY SIGNATURE	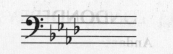
SIXTEENTH/EIGHTH/ SIXTEENTH NOTE COMBINATION		

29 **Ab MAJOR SCALE SKILL**

30 **ARTICULATION ADVENTURE**

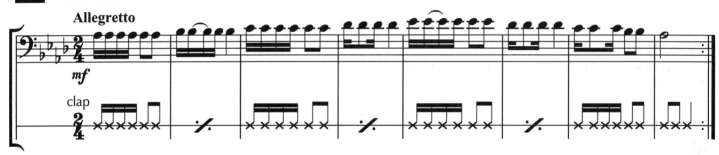

▶ Write in the counting for the top line before you play.

31 **LA RASPA**

Mexican Folk Song

32 **TECHNIQUE BREAK**

33 **LONDONDERRY AIR - Band Arrangement** Page 44 ▶ Irish Folk Song
arr. Bruce Pearson (b. 1942)

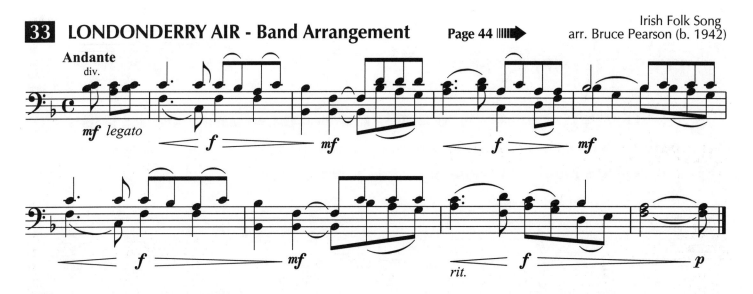

34 **TECHNIQUE BREAK**

35 _____ Composer _____
your name

▶ Compose a song that is shaped like the curved lines. Title and play your composition.

36 **PENTATONIC SCALES**

▶ Pentatonic scales consist of five notes. Two forms of the pentatonic scale are shown above.

37 **GO FOR EXCELLENCE!** Korean Folk Song

▶ "Arirang" is based on a pentatonic scale.

W23TB

D MINOR KEY SIGNATURE		**D minor** has the same key signature as **F major**.
TEMPO		**Andantino -** Faster than **Andante**, but not as fast as **Moderato**.

38 WARM-UP - Band Arrangement Page 44 ▶

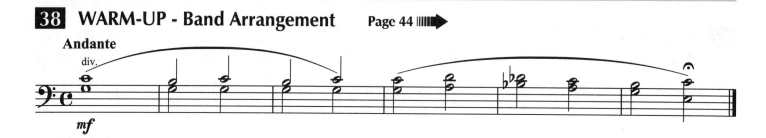

39 D MINOR SCALE SKILL

40 TECHNIQUE BREAK

41 FOR TROMBONES ONLY

SIXTEENTH REST

$\frac{7}{}$ = ¼ count in $\frac{2}{4}$, $\frac{3}{4}$, and $\frac{4}{4}$ time.

A sixteenth rest is as long as a sixteenth note.

42 TINGA LAYO

West Indies Folk Song

Moderato

mf

Fine

D.C. al Fine

© M. Baron Co. Used by permission.

43 HWI NE YA HE

American Indian Song

Allegro

f

44 SIXTEENTH STUDY

A **Andantino** **B** **C**

mf

D **E** **F**

▶ Write in the counting and clap the rhythm before you play.

45 GO FOR EXCELLENCE!

French Canadian Folk Song

Allegretto

"Envoyons D'L'Avant, Nos Gens!"

mp

▶ Name the key in "Go For Excellence!" _____

W23TB

THE MIDDLE AGES (400 - 1400)

DOTTED QUARTER REST

A dot after a rest adds half the value of the rest.

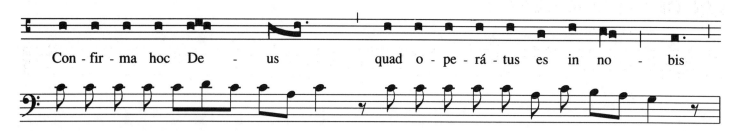

46 **CONFIRMA HOC**

Plainsong

Con - fir - ma hoc De - us   quad o - pe - rá - tus es in no - bis

▶ Keep the eighth notes even at all times.

© G.I.A. Publications, Inc. Used by permission.

47 **DESCENDIT DE COELIS**

Notre Dame Organum

48 **ESTAMPIE**

Anonymous

49 **SUMER IS ICUMEN IN**   Page 44 ▉▉▶

English Round

THE RENAISSANCE (1400 - 1600)

D♭ MAJOR KEY SIGNATURE

This key signature means play all B's as B flats, all E's as E flats, all A's as A flats, all D's as D flats, and all G's as G flats.

50 D♭ MAJOR SCALE SKILL

Andantino · Arpeggio · Chords

51 VOX DILECTI MEI - Band Arrangement

Palestrina (1525 - 1594)
arr. Bruce Pearson (b. 1942)

52 TECHNIQUE BREAK

Andantino · *mp* · *mf simile* · *f* · *mf*

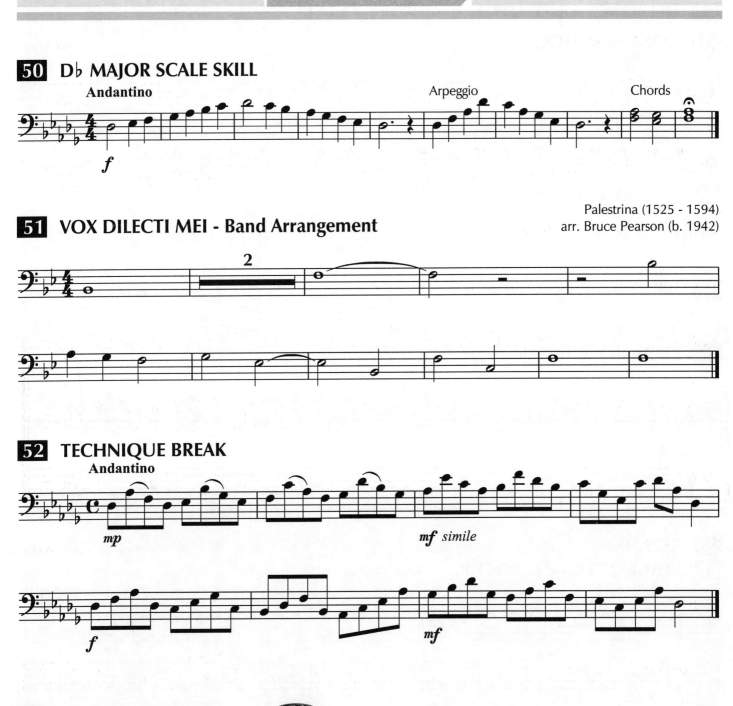

53 GO FOR EXCELLENCE!

"The Official Branle"

Thoinot Arbeau (1520 - 1595)

THE RENAISSANCE, continued

ENHARMONICS

G# = Ab

54 OLD ONE HUNDREDTH - Band Arrangement

Louis Bourgeois (c. 1510 - c. 1561)
arr. Bruce Pearson (b. 1942)

div.

55 NOW IS THE MONTH OF MAYING

Thomas Morley (1557 - 1602)

56 TECHNIQUE BREAK

Allegro

mf

simile

57 BERGERETTE SANS ROCHE   Page 44 ▶▶▶

Basse Danse
Tielman Susato (c. 1500 - c. 1561)

© MUSIKit Recorder, Roger and Carol Buckton, The Recorder Centre. Used by permission.

58 FOR TROMBONES ONLY

Allegro

G#

mf

▶ Try to play this exercise with one breath.

EARLE OF OXFORDS MARCHE

Band Arrangement

William Byrd (1543 - 1623)
arr. Bruce Pearson (b. 1942)

59 _____   Arranger _____

your name

▶ Create fauxbourdon by writing a duet part a sixth below this Renaissance melody. Title your composition, and play the top part while a friend plays the bottom part.

60 **GO FOR EXCELLENCE!**

THE BAROQUE PERIOD (1600 - 1750)

61 BALANCE BUILDER

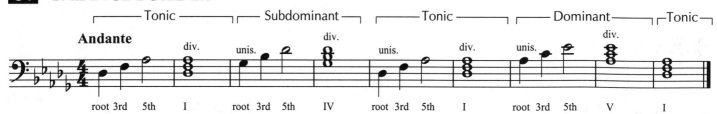

62 TRUMPET TUNE

Henry Purcell (1659 - 1695)

63 LE PETIT RIEN

François Couperin (1668 - 1733)

▶ When you see a staccato note at the end of a slur, slur to the note but make it short.

64 FOR TROMBONES ONLY

 Page 45 ▶

W23TB

TIME SIGNATURE	$\frac{9}{8}$	$\frac{9}{8}$ = 9 counts in each measure $\frac{9}{8}$ = eighth note gets 1 count

STYLE	*grazioso* - gracefully

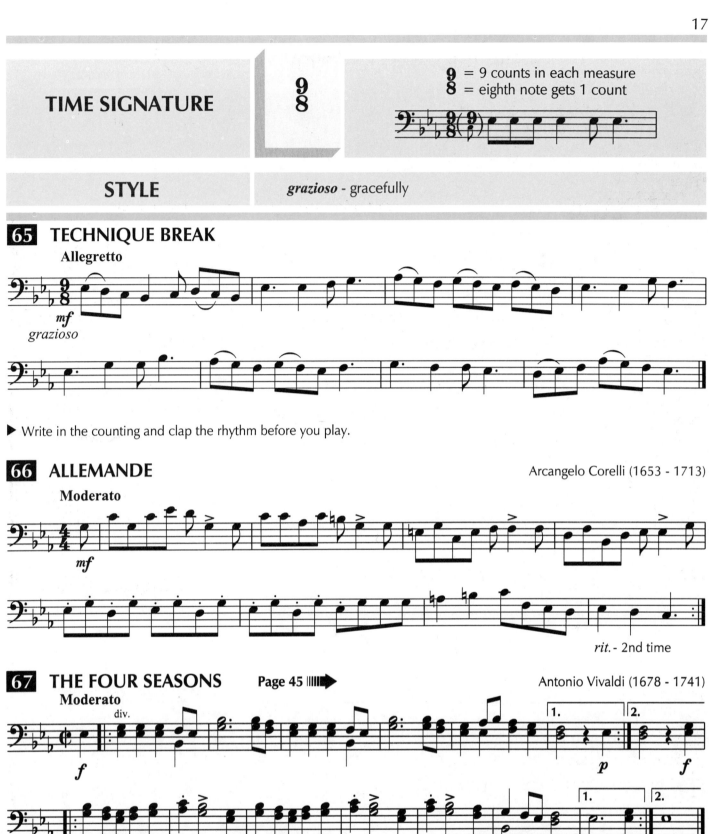

65 TECHNIQUE BREAK

Allegretto

mf
grazioso

▶ Write in the counting and clap the rhythm before you play.

66 ALLEMANDE   Arcangelo Corelli (1653 - 1713)

Moderato

mf

rit. - 2nd time

67 THE FOUR SEASONS   Page 45 ▶   Antonio Vivaldi (1678 - 1741)

Moderato

div.

f   *p*   *f*

rit. - 2nd time   *p*

68 GO FOR EXCELLENCE!   Johann Sebastian Bach (1685 - 1750)

Moderato

"Jesu, Joy of Man's Desiring"

mp grazioso

rit.

THE BAROQUE PERIOD, continued

69 **CHORALE - Band Arrangement**

Hans Leo Hassler (c. 1562 - 1612)
arr. Bruce Pearson (b. 1942)

70 **HORNPIPE FROM "WATER MUSIC SUITE"**

George Frideric Handel (1685 - 1759)

71 **TECHNIQUE BREAK**

72 **FANTASIA CHROMATICA**

Johann Sebastian Bach (1685 - 1750)

73 **FOR TROMBONES ONLY**

▶ Continue playing this lip slur pattern using the following slide positions: **4; 5; 6; 7.**

SIXTEENTH NOTES IN 3/8, 6/8, & 9/8 TIME

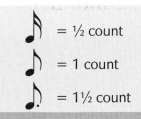

A single sixteenth note is half as long as an eighth note.

74 ARTICULATION ADVENTURE

Moderato

mf

▶ Write in the counting and clap the rhythm before you play.

75 MINUETTO   Domenico Scarlatti (1685 - 1757)

Allegretto

mp grazioso   *cresc.*   *mf*   *decresc.*

mp cresc.   *mf*

▶ *cresc.* (◁———) - gradually play louder. *decresc.* (———▷) - gradually play softer.

76 PASSEPIED   Page 45 ▐▐▐▐▶   Georg Philipp Telemann (1681 - 1767)

Allegro

f - 1st time
p - 2nd time

f - 1st time
p - 2nd time

77 GO FOR EXCELLENCE!   George Frideric Handel (1685 - 1759)

Andantino

"Siciliana from Music for the Royal Fireworks"

p legato   *f*   *mf*

cresc.   *f decresc.*   *mp*

W23TB

THE BAROQUE PERIOD, continued

78 TECHNIQUE BREAK

▶ Name the key in "Technique Break." _____

REJOUISSANCE
from Music for the Royal Fireworks
Band Arrangement

George Frideric Handel (1685 - 1759)
arr. Bruce Pearson (b. 1942)

THE CLASSICAL PERIOD (1750-1820)

GRACE NOTE	TEMPO	STYLE
A small-sized note played just before the note to which it is attached.	**Larghetto -** not as slow as **Largo**	*dolce* - sweetly

79 **THEME FROM PIANO SONATA NO. 2** Wolfgang Amadeus Mozart (1756 - 1791)

Larghetto

80 **GERMAN DANCE** Franz Joseph Haydn (1732 - 1809)

Allegretto

81 **TECHNIQUE BREAK**

Moderato

82 **GO FOR EXCELLENCE!** Ludwig van Beethoven (1770 - 1827)

Larghetto

"Sonatina"

W23TB

THE CLASSICAL PERIOD, continued

| BINARY FORM | AB | Music that has two different sections. |

83 **AUSTRIAN HYMN - Band Arrangement**   Page 45 ▶   Franz Joseph Haydn (1732 - 1809) arr. Bruce Pearson (b. 1942)

84 **RUSSIAN FOLK SONG**   Ludwig van Beethoven (1770 - 1827)

85 **TECHNIQUE BREAK**

accel. - 2nd time

86 **FOR TROMBONES ONLY**

▶ Play each pattern four times. Start slowly and increase speed.

TERNARY FORM	ABA	The A section is followed by the B section, and then the A section is played again.

87 SCOTCH DANCE

Ludwig van Beethoven (1770 - 1827)

▶ Name the form used in "Scotch Dance." _____

88 TECHNIQUE BREAK

Rodolphe Kreutzer (1766 - 1831)

89 GO FOR EXCELLENCE!

Wolfgang Amadeus Mozart (1756 - 1791)

"Theme from Symphony No. 40"

THE CLASSICAL PERIOD, continued

RONDO FORM	ABACA	The main section A returns several times and alternates with other sections.

90 CADENCES Page 45 ▐▐▐▶

RONDO

Band Arrangement

Franz Joseph Haydn (1732 - 1809)
arr. Bruce Pearson (b. 1942)

THE ROMANTIC PERIOD (1820 - 1900)

F MINOR KEY SIGNATURE	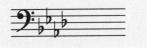	**F minor** has the same key signature as **A♭ major.**

91 CAST THY BURDEN FROM "ELIJAH" - Band Arrangement

Felix Mendelssohn (1809 - 1847)
arr. Bruce Pearson (b. 1942)

92 F MINOR SCALE SKILL Page 45 ▶

93 TECHNIQUE BREAK

▶ Try playing both octaves.

94 GO FOR EXCELLENCE!

Johannes Brahms (1833 - 1897)

"Hungarian Dance No. 5"

THE ROMANTIC PERIOD, continued

TIME SIGNATURE	$\frac{6}{4}$	**6** = 6 counts in each measure **4** = quarter note gets 1 count

DAL SEGNO AL CODA (D.S. AL CODA)	Go back to the segno sign (𝄋) and play until the coda sign. When you reach the coda sign, skip to the *Coda.*

95 SCHEHERAZADE   Nicolai Rimsky-Korsakov (1844 - 1908)

Andantino 𝄋

p grazioso

to Coda ⊕

mp

D.S. al Coda

⊕ *Coda*

rit. ——— *pp*

96 LAUGHING SONG FROM "DIE FLEDERMAUS"   Johann Strauss, Jr. (1825 - 1899)

Allegretto

mp

▶ Write in the counting and clap the rhythm before you play.

97 FIRE FESTIVAL POLKA   Page 45 ▐▐▐▶   Josef Strauss (1827 - 1870)

Moderato

f

p

1.

2.

——— *mf*   ——— *f*

98 FOR TROMBONES ONLY

Moderato

mf

1   2   3   4   5   6   1

W23TB

TIME SIGNATURE	$\frac{5}{4}$	G MAJOR KEY SIGNATURE	STYLE
$\frac{5}{4}$ = 5 counts in each measure = quarter note gets 1 count		This key signature means play all F's as F sharps.	*sostenuto-* sustained

99 TECHNIQUE BREAK
Moderato

▶ Write in the counting and clap the rhythm before you play.

100 G MAJOR SCALE SKILL　　Page 46 ▶

Andante

Arpeggio *mf*

Chords
div.

▶ Try playing both octaves.

101 PILGRIMS CHORUS FROM "TANNHAUSER"　　Richard Wagner (1813 - 1883)

Andante

mp sostenuto

cresc.

f　　*mp*　*f*　　*mp*

102 GO FOR EXCELLENCE!　　Modeste Mussorgsky (1839 - 1881)
Maestoso
"Promenade from Pictures at an Exhibition"

f sostenuto

rit.　*ff*

W23TB

THE ROMANTIC PERIOD, continued

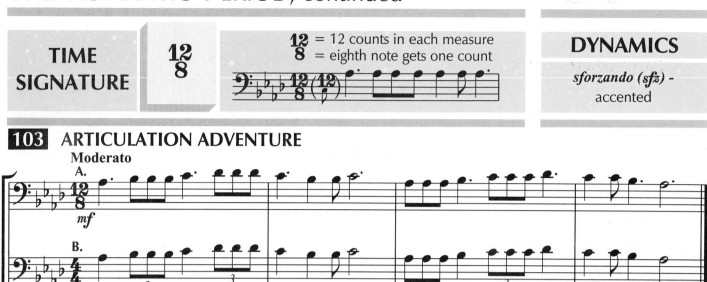

TIME SIGNATURE	12/8	12/8 = 12 counts in each measure / eighth note gets one count	DYNAMICS

sforzando (sfz) - accented

103 ARTICULATION ADVENTURE

Moderato

▶ Write in the counting and clap the rhythm before you play.

104 TECHNIQUE BREAK

Carl Czerny (1791 - 1857)

Moderato

105 THE WILD HORSEMAN

Robert Schumann (1810 - 1856)

A Moderato

B

▶ Line A is in the key of G minor. On line B, write in the melody a whole step lower to transpose to the key of F minor. Play both lines.

106 FOR TROMBONES ONLY Page 46 ▸

ta ka ta ka ta / da ga da ga da

▶ Experiment using the syllables indicated to learn double tonguing. Practice slowly at first, increasing speed as you become more proficient. Use whatever set of syllables works best for you.

STYLE	*cantabile* - in a singing style

ENHARMONICS

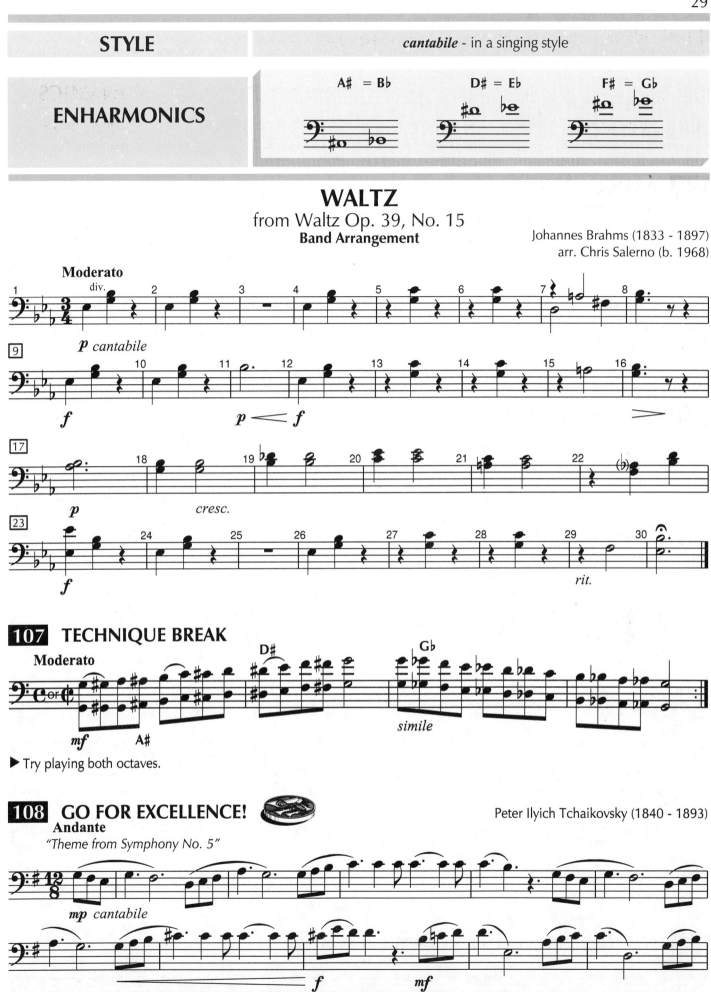

WALTZ
from Waltz Op. 39, No. 15
Band Arrangement

Johannes Brahms (1833 - 1897)
arr. Chris Salerno (b. 1968)

107 TECHNIQUE BREAK

▶ Try playing both octaves.

108 GO FOR EXCELLENCE!

Peter Ilyich Tchaikovsky (1840 - 1893)

"Theme from Symphony No. 5"

20th CENTURY ART MUSIC

| A MINOR KEY SIGNATURE | | **A minor** has the same key signature as **C major**. |

109 A MINOR SCALE SKILL

110 PAVANE Page 47 — Gabriel Fauré (1845 - 1924)

111 WHOLE-TONE SCALE STUDY

▶ A whole-tone scale consists of only whole steps.

112 EXCERPT FROM "PRELUDE TO THE AFTERNOON OF A FAUN" Impressionism Example Claude Debussy (1862 - 1918)

▶ This piece is based on a whole-tone scale.

113 THE SUNKEN CATHEDRAL - Band Arrangement Impressionism Example Claude Debussy (1862 - 1918) arr. Chuck Elledge (b. 1961))

▶ This piece demonstrates a technique called planing, where all notes of a chord move the same direction. This is also called parallel motion.

ASYMMETRICAL METERS

Meters or time signatures with an uneven number of eighth notes (usually $\frac{3}{8}$, $\frac{5}{8}$, or $\frac{7}{8}$).

114 FOLK MELODY A LA BÉLA BARTÓK (1881 - 1945)

Nationalism Example
Stephen Foster (1826 - 1864)
arr. Chris Salerno (b. 1968)

115 ODE TO IGOR STRAVINSKY (1882 - 1971) - Band Arrangement

Primitivism Example
arr. Chris Salerno (b. 1968)

116 TECHNIQUE BREAK

▶ Write in the counting and clap the rhythm before you play.

117 GO FOR EXCELLENCE!

Claude Debussy (1862 - 1918)

Allegro

"Golliwog's Cake Walk from Children's Corner"

W23TB

20th CENTURY ART MUSIC, continued

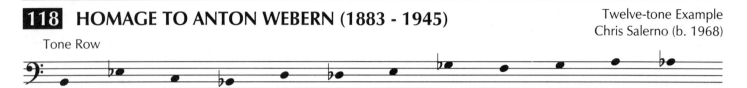

DYNAMICS	*forte-piano* (*fp*) - loud, then immediately soft

118 **HOMAGE TO ANTON WEBERN (1883 - 1945)**

Twelve-tone Example
Chris Salerno (b. 1968)

Tone Row

▶ Notice that the tone row uses all twelve notes of the chromatic scale once.

119 **TONE ROW**

120 _____ Composer _____

your name

▶ Compose a twelve-tone composition. Title and play your composition.

121 **FOR TROMBONES ONLY**

Page 47 ▐▐▐▐➡

ta	ta	ka	ta
ta	ka	ta	ta
da	da	ga	da
da	ga	da	da

▶ Experiment using the syllables indicated to learn triple tonguing. Practice slowly at first, increasing speed as you become more proficient. Use whatever set of syllables works best for you.

WAR
from The Four Horsemen
Band Arrangement

Andrew Boysen, Jr. (b. 1968)

122 TRIBUTE TO CHARLES IVES (1874 - 1954)

Bitonal Example
Stephen Foster (1826 - 1864)
arr. Chris Salerno (b. 1968)

123 GO FOR EXCELLENCE!

W23TB

20th CENTURY POP MUSIC

QUARTER NOTE TRIPLET

$\frac{2}{3} + \frac{2}{3} + \frac{2}{3} = 2$ counts in $\frac{2}{4}$, $\frac{3}{4}$, and $\frac{4}{4}$ time.

124 SEMPER FIDELIS
Allegro
Music of the Band Tradition
John Philip Sousa (1854 - 1932)
A. Melody
B. Countermelody

125 THE EASY WINNERS Page 47 ▶
Allegretto
Ragtime Example
Scott Joplin (1868 - 1917)

126 TRIPLETS, TRIPLETS, TRIPLETS
Moderato

127 TECHNIQUE BREAK
Allegretto

▶ Write in the counting and clap the rhythm before you play.
W23TB

STYLE

Swing - played as

TWO-MEASURE REPEAT SIGN

Repeat the two previous measures.

128 SWINGING BLUES SCALE

129 SWINGING BLUES CHORD PROGRESSION (Arpeggios)

130 BLUES CHORD ACCOMPANIMENT - Band Arrangement

▶ This exercise can be played with 131 and 132.

131 TIN ROOF BLUES   Traditional Blues Example

132 GO FOR EXCELLENCE!

"Blues for a Fat Cat"

W23TB

20th CENTURY POP MUSIC, continued

133 **'55 T-BIRD** **Page 47** ⮕

1950s Rock and Roll Example
Kevin Daley (b. 1957)

Moderato

134 **RIGHT ON**

1970s Rock Example
Kevin Daley (b. 1957)

Allegretto

▶ Write in the counting and clap the rhythm before you play.

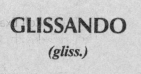
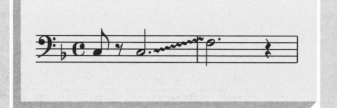

JAMBALAYA JAMMIN'

Band Arrangement

W23TB

SCALE STUDIES

1 **B♭ MAJOR SCALE**

2 **G HARMONIC MINOR SCALE**

3 **E♭ MAJOR SCALE**

4 **C HARMONIC MINOR SCALE**

SCALE STUDIES

5 **F MAJOR SCALE**

6 **D HARMONIC MINOR SCALE**

7 **A♭ MAJOR SCALE**

8 **F HARMONIC MINOR SCALE**

Page 40

SCALE STUDIES

9 C MAJOR SCALE

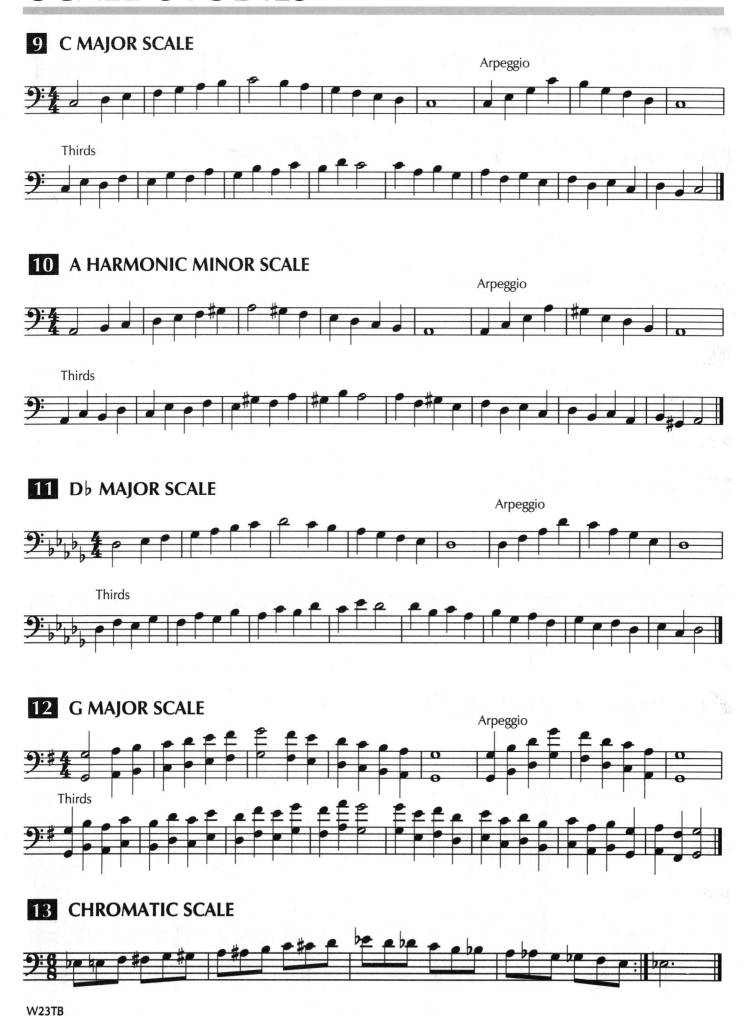

10 A HARMONIC MINOR SCALE

11 D♭ MAJOR SCALE

12 G MAJOR SCALE

13 CHROMATIC SCALE

W23TB

RHYTHM STUDIES

RHYTHM STUDIES

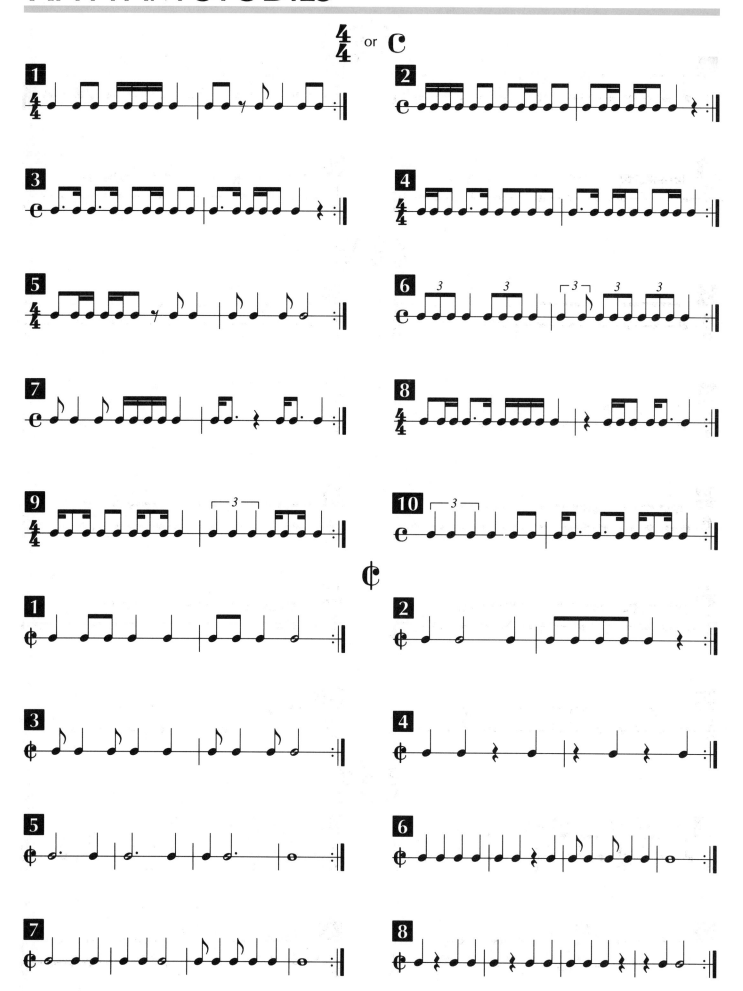

RHYTHM STUDIES

EXCELLERATORS-For Trombones Only

▶ Try to play this exercise with one breath.

▶ Play each of the lip slur patterns using the following slide positions: **1; 2; 3; 4; 5; 6; 7.**

45

EXCELLERATORS-FOR TROMBONES ONLY

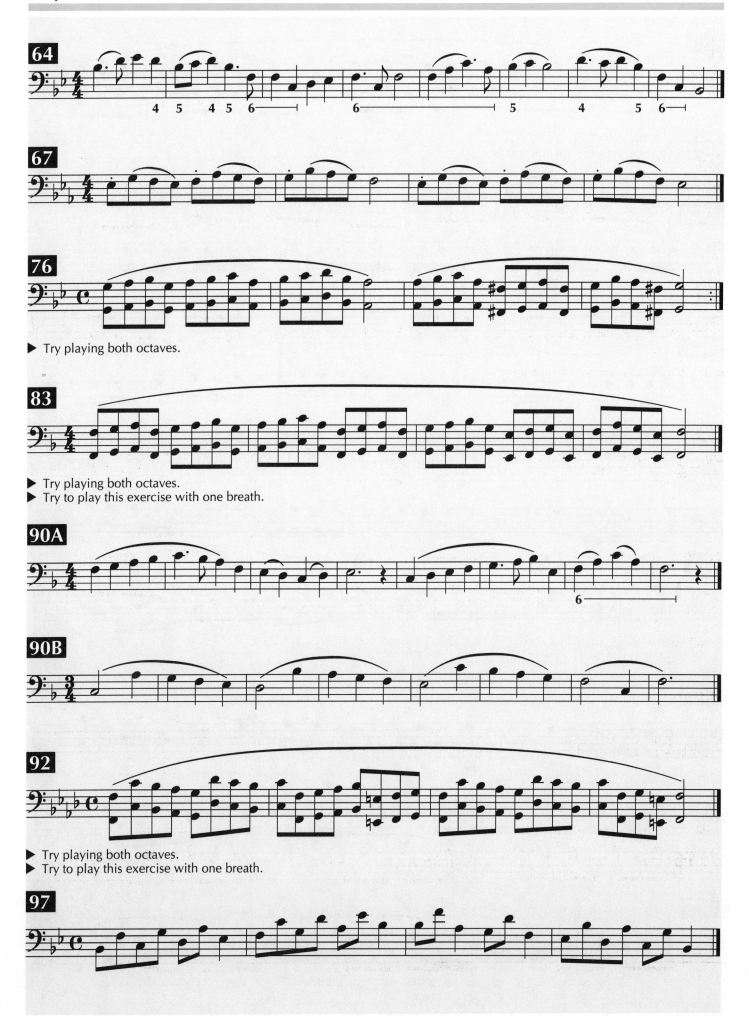

▶ Try playing both octaves.

▶ Try playing both octaves.
▶ Try to play this exercise with one breath.

▶ Try playing both octaves.
▶ Try to play this exercise with one breath.

EXCELLERATORS-FOR TROMBONES ONLY

100

▶ Try playing both octaves.
▶ Try to play this exercise with one breath.

106A

ta ka ta ka ta ka ta ka ta *simile*
da ga da ga da ga da ga da

106B

ta ka ta ka ta *simile*
da ga da ga da

106C

ta ka ta ka ta *simile*
da ga da ga da

106D

ta   ta ka ta *simile*
da   da ga da

106E

ta ka ta ka ta ka ta ka ta ka ta ka ta *simile*
da ga da ga da ga da ga da ga da ga da

EXCELLERATORS-For Trombones Only

110

▶ Continue playing this lip slur pattern using the following slide positions: **4; 5; 6; 7.**

121A

ta ta ka ta ta ka ta
ta ka ta ta ka ta ta
da da ga da da ga da
da ga da da ga da da

simile

121B

ta ta ka ta ta ka ta
ta ka ta ta ka ta ta
da da ga da da ga da
da ga da da ga da da

simile

121C

ta ta ka ta ta ka ta
ta ka ta ta ka ta ta
da da ga da da ga da
da ga da da ga da da

simile

125

133

TROMBONE POSITION CHART

+ = Slightly extend the slide
- = Slightly shorten the slide